GRADE LEVEL 5.5
BOOK
NUMBER 24642
POINTS 1.0

W9-ANM-408

	DATE DUE		

796.72
MCK   McKenna, A. T.

Stock Car Racing

449599

–Fast Tracks

–Stock Car Racing

A.T. McKenna

H C STORM SCHOOL

visit us at
www.abdopub.com

Published by Abdo & Daughters, 4940 Viking Drive, Suite 622, Edina, Minnesota 55435.
Copyright © 1998 by Abdo Consulting Group, Inc., Pentagon Tower, P.O. Box 36036, Minneapolis, Minnesota 55435 USA. International copyrights reserved in all countries. No part of this book may be reproduced in any form without written permission from the publisher.

Printed in the United States.

Cover and Interior Photo credits: Allsport USA, Duomo, SportsChrome

Edited by Paul Joseph

Library of Congress Cataloging-in-Publication Data

McKenna, A. T.
    Stock car racing / A. T. McKenna.
       p.   cm. -- (Fast tracks)
   Includes index.
   Summary: Provides a simple introduction to stock car racing, describing the cars and their special features, the drivers and their training, and a day at the races.
    ISBN 1-56239-837-7
   1. Stock car racing--Juvenile literature.   [1. Stock car racing.]
   I. Title II. Series: McKenna, A.T. Fast tracks.
   GV1029.9.S74M35 1998
   796.72'0973--dc21

                                     97-28477
                                         CIP
                                         AC

–Contents

-Stock Car Racing

Stock Car racing is one of the most popular types of auto racing in the United States today. In the beginning, stock car racing took place all over the country. Drivers modified their regular, everyday cars, and competed against one another for speed. Larger, more powerful engines were placed inside and wider wheels with much larger tires were used. Drivers raced in informal races on county roads and at the fairgrounds. State and county fairgrounds worked well for auto racing, since there were tracks already there for horse racing. At first, these competitions involved only those who were racing. But gradually spectators began to attend and prize money was awarded to the winner of the race.

In February of 1948, the National Association for Stock Car Auto Racing (NASCAR) was formed. NASCAR is called a sanctioning body, which means the organization sets the rules for racing, including how the cars are built.

NASCAR also decides the prize money for the winners and sets up a point system that determines which driver is the national champion at the end of the racing season. Drivers receive a certain number of points at each race, depending on which spot

they finish. The driver with the most points at the end of the season is named national champion. NASCAR calls its racing series the Winston Cup Series.

NASCAR sets the standards for how a stock car is to be built.

-Building the Cars

From the outside, a stock car looks much like many of the cars being driven on the streets everyday. Some of the more popular stock cars raced today are the Chevrolet Monte Carlo, the Pontiac Grand Prix, and the Ford Thunderbird. The Thunderbird is the oldest body style still being raced. However, stock cars don't look much like a regular car once you look inside.

The first component on a stock car is the chassis or roll cage. The chassis looks like the skeleton of a car. The chassis consists of several pieces of steel welded together to form a frame for the car. All sharp edges on the chassis must be smoothed before putting them together. All pieces must fit perfectly in order for the chassis to work. The chassis must be very strong to protect the driver if there is a crash.

Next, a body is placed on the chassis. The body is made of stock sheet metal. Most of the body is made by hand by the car builder. The roof, rear deck, and hood of the car are usually the only pieces that come from the manufacturers such as Ford, Chevrolet, and Chrysler. These three pieces are what make the cars look like regular cars driven on the road. When the body is all complete, you can't see any gaps or spaces in between the body pieces. The car looks like it is all one piece.

Most of a stock car is hand-made to look like one piece.

-Inside a Stock Car

After the chassis and body are welded together, the inside parts are then added. These include the engine, fuel system, exhaust system, and cooling system.

The engine size is limited to 358 cubic inches. These engines are rated at about 700 horsepower, which means the cars can race around the track at speeds of 200 miles per hour (322 kilometers per hour) and higher. The only type of engine allowed in a stock car is called a small block V-8.

Stock cars have large fuel tanks, which are called fuel cells. The fuel cell has a steel body and an internal bladder, or lining, which is much stronger than a fuel tank on a regular car. This makes the fuel cell much harder to damage and prevents fuel from splattering out if there is a crash. The fuel cell can carry 22 gallons of fuel.

On a regular car, the exhaust pipes are found in the rear of the car, between the rear wheels, most times on the passenger's side. On a stock car, the exhaust pipes are on either side of the car, between the front and rear wheel. Some teams place one exhaust pipe on each side of the car. Many teams place both pipes on the left side of the car, so the pipes won't be blocked if the car turns and brushes against the wall of the track.

During the race, the engine gets very hot. Grill openings in the front of the car help supply cool air to the engine area. The cooling system helps cool down the radiator and also the brakes with electric fans. The driver also gets quite hot inside the cockpit. Air vents and fans help keep the driver cool, too.

Jeff Gordon at the 1996 Goodyear 500 auto race.

–Tons of Tires

Racing tires and wheels are larger than those on a regular car. This helps to keep the car steady when going around a sharp curve or passing another car. Tire pressure, or how much air you put in the tire, can make a big difference in the performance of the car. The more pressure in the tire, the stiffer the tire becomes. A different amount of tire pressure is put in each of the four tires to help the car handle the best on the track.

Tires wear out very quickly during a race. They are replaced several times with new, warm tires that are kept heated in an electric covering, much like a blanket. Warm tires grip the track better and allow the driver to go faster. Sometimes a team can go through over a dozen sets of tires during the race weekend. A set of four race tires can cost about $1,300 each. Teams buy their tires at the track from Goodyear. Goodyear mounts and balances the tires for many teams.

Tires must be changed several times during a single race.

<u>-Stop!</u>

In order to win a race, you eventually have to stop! The brakes are a very important part of a stock car. The driver needs to use the brakes when going around a turn or when pulling over for a tire change. Inside the car, the brake pedal is placed very close to the accelerator (gas pedal) so the driver can use the heel of the foot to brake, and the toes to increase speed. While racing, there is no time to take the foot completely off the brake and then put it on the gas pedal. The driver must do both at the same time. This is the "heel/toe" system.

Stock car brakes are much stronger than regular brakes. The brakes must be made to stand up to the heat that is created when a driver must brake fast. The stock car brake pads are also very strong. The brake pads are made of a carbon/

Driver Terry Labonte taking a pit stop.

metal mix, which helps stand up to the heat and prevents the pads from wearing out too quickly. One set of brake pads usually lasts an entire race.

−From the Driver's Seat

The interior of a stock car doesn't look anything like a regular car. Most of the changes are made for the safety and protection of the driver. The roll bars, which are part of the roll cage or chassis, are padded with foam inside the driver's area. The gear shifter is also padded to prevent injury. The driver's area must include a Halon fire extinguishing system. Gauges, which show the gas, oil, and water levels, are large and placed in a spot where the driver can easily see them.

The steering wheel on a stock car is a "quick-release" steering wheel, which means it comes off fast, if needed. A pull on a pin and a tug on the steering wheel are all it takes to make extra space so the driver can easily get out of the car.

All of the seats in the car are removed except for the driver's. The driver has a special bucket-style seat that fits the driver's body snugly. This type of seat is more comfortable when the car is traveling at high speeds. The seat is made of aluminum pieces with padding to protect the ribs and a special padded headrest. The headrest will help prevent injuries to the neck and head in case of an accident. A seat belt, called a safety harness, makes sure the driver won't be moved out of place.

Stock car driver Bill Elliott at the starting line.

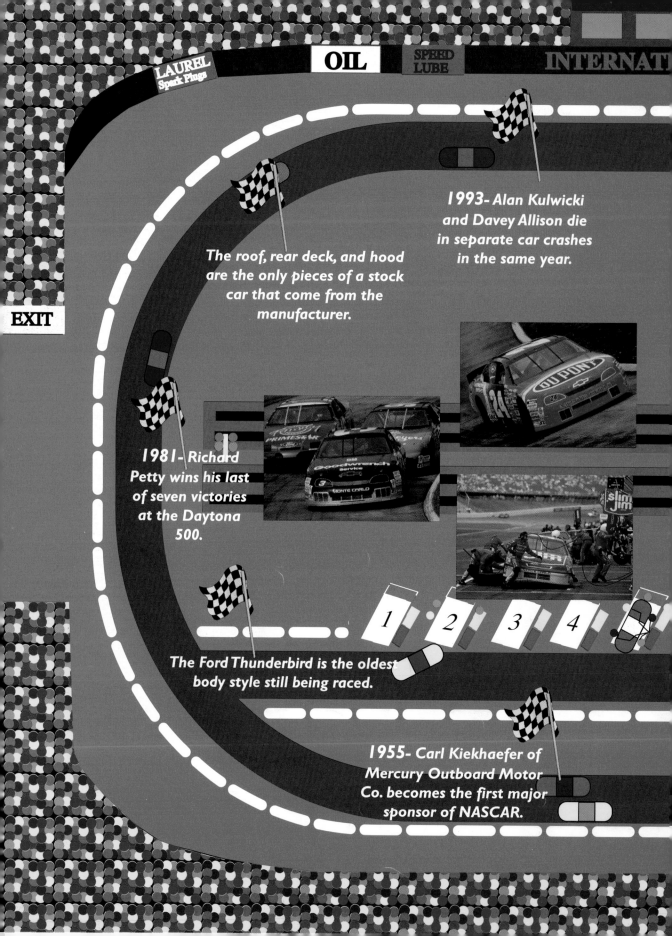

LAUREL
Spark Plugs

OIL

SPEED
LUBE

INTERNATI

EXIT

The roof, rear deck, and hood
are the only pieces of a stock
car that come from the
manufacturer.

1993- Alan Kulwicki
and Davey Allison die
in separate car crashes
in the same year.

1981- Richard
Petty wins his last
of seven victories
at the Daytona
500.

1   2   3   4

The Ford Thunderbird is the oldest
body style still being raced.

1955- Carl Kiekhaefer of
Mercury Outboard Motor
Co. becomes the first major
sponsor of NASCAR.

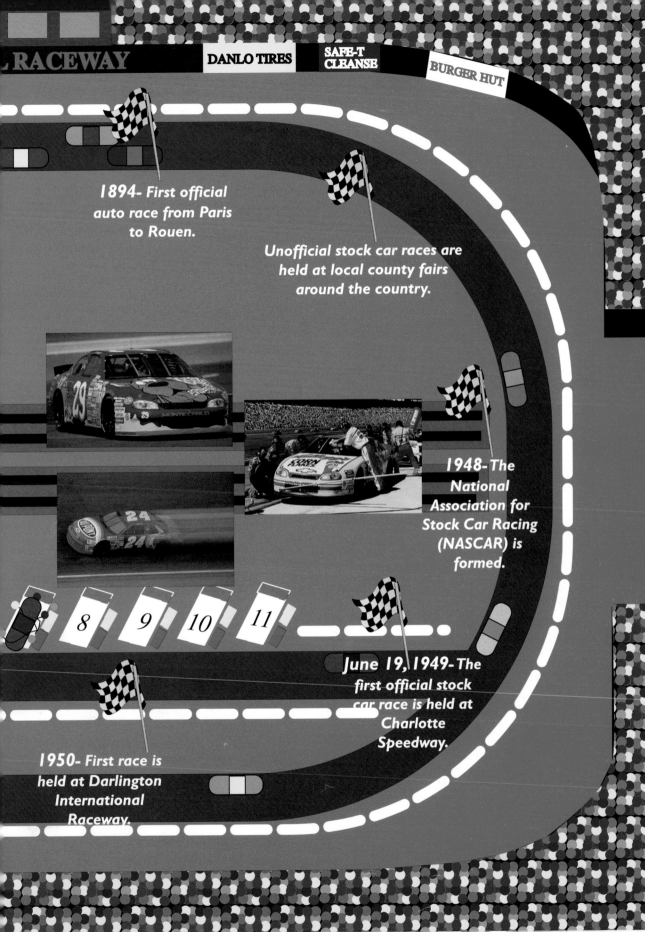

1894- First official auto race from Paris to Rouen.

Unofficial stock car races are held at local county fairs around the country.

1948- The National Association for Stock Car Racing (NASCAR) is formed.

8   9   10   11

June 19, 1949- The first official stock car race is held at Charlotte Speedway.

1950- First race is held at Darlington International Raceway.

All glass on the sides and back window of the car is removed. The driver's side window must have a nylon window net instead. This window net can be quickly removed if the driver needs to get out of the car. The right side window must be enclosed with safety glass. The small side quarter windows are made of a sturdy material called Lexan. The front windshield is made of a hard coated polycarbonate material. Strips of metal hold the front and back windshields in place.

Once the body of the car is assembled, the car is given a paint job. Stock cars are brightly painted, with the names and labels of the companies who help to pay for the car. These companies are called sponsors.

Some of the names seen on stock cars include companies that make car products such as Goodyear, Shell, STP, Phillips 66, Firestone, DieHard, and Quaker State. The driver's name is painted above the driver's side window.

Rules specify where the car number should be displayed on the car and the minimum size the number must be. The car number is painted on both sides of the car and on the roof of the car so it can be seen from all angles, even the official's tower above the track. When these brightly colored cars race by on the track at full speed, all that can be seen is a rainbow of colors.

–Driver Gear

Every bit of clothing the driver wears must be made of special safety materials. Drivers must wear driving suits that are fireproof and usually made of a material called Nomex. Socks, gloves, shoes, even underwear must also be fireproof. This is to protect the driver in the case of an engine fire while driving or during a crash.

A high-quality helmet is one of the most important pieces of the driver's gear. The helmet could save a driver's life during a crash. The helmet has a radio attached so the driver can communicate with the crew during the race. The driver can say 'I'm coming in for a tire change,' and the crew will be ready. There are also vents in the helmet to keep the driver cool. Most helmets are brightly painted in the driver's favorite colors, or painted to match the car colors.

Stock cars are so fast that all you see as they drive by is a blur of color.

—Learning to Drive

Becoming a professional stock car racer takes practice and years of experience. Most famous stock car drivers either went to a driving school, or started out racing at their local tracks. Some of the entry level stock car classes are Street Stock, Hobby Stock, and Mini Stock.

Driving schools supply students with the cars, helmets, driving suits, and instructors. Most schools require that a student is at least 18 years old and has a valid driver's license. At a driving school, the student is taught to drive the car safely at a fast speed. This is the best place to decide if race car driving is right for you.

Local stock car tracks have information on the different beginner series of stock car racing. Many times you must have your own car to race, but some tracks will have cars available to rent, depending on the series. Many stock car drivers actually started out in kart racing. This gives a driver the chance to start racing at a young age.

Opposite page: Daytona International Speedway is one of the most famous racetracks.

–At the Track

Most stock car tracks are called ovals. The cars race around the tracks in one direction, counter-clockwise. The tracks have very wide corners that are on a slope or slant. These are called banked curves. Drivers can choose to go around the curves at a high, medium, or low level. Most of the crashes and bumping into the walls happens on the curves. The walls are made of solid concrete and have a fence on top to protect the people watching the race.

The long length of the track is called the straight-away. This is the area where the driver can really pick up speed. The start/finish line is located in the middle of the straight-away.

Probably the most famous of all stock car race tracks is Daytona International Speedway. This track was opened in 1959 by Bill France, one of the co-founders of NASCAR. The banked oval track is 2-1/2 miles (4 km) around. The Daytona 500 race, held every year, is a race of 500 miles on this track.

-Qualifying Day

Qualifying day usually takes place on the Friday before the race. During this time, the driver and crew chief work closely together to get the best spot in the lineup of cars for the race on Sunday. The crew chief is in charge of the pit crew and helping to prepare the car. The crew chief also works with the engine builder to help gain a competitive edge. The pit crew is made up of team members who change tires and add fuel to the car during the race.

During qualifying, the driver takes two fast laps around the track. Drivers compete for the fastest qualifying speed, which will determine their spot in the lineup. The driver is allowed two chances, or two qualifying laps around the track on qualifying day.

The driver with the fastest qualifying time is called the pole sitter. This driver will start the race in the front row. Those who do not qualify well or crash during qualifying end up at the very end of the line. There are a certain amount of spots available for any race. Not every driver will get a spot in the lineup.

–Practice Day

Saturday is spent setting up the car and practicing for the race the following day. This day is very critical to drivers. It is the last chance the driver will have to race around the track until the race. It is also the last chance the race team will have to set up the car before the race. This includes working on the engine, brakes, and handling of the car.

Two cars are taken to the track for a race weekend. One is the primary car driven, and the other is a backup. The backup car is used in case the primary car gets damaged during practice or qualifying. If the primary car was damaged during qualifying, practice day is the only day the team has to work on this extra car to get it ready for the big race.

Before a driver can compete on the race track, the driver must pass an inspection by the race officials. Rules are very strict. If an item on the car is the wrong size, or made out of the wrong material, the car can be disqualified from the race. The car may be taken away and the driver may have to pay a fine. Rules about the cars are made for the safety of the drivers and to make sure each driver is given a fair chance at competition.

Opposite page: When trying to qualify, the faster your speed the better starting position you get.

One of the inspections is weighing the car with electric scales. Stock cars are not lightweight. They tip the scales at 3,600 pounds (1633 kg). The height of the car is also measured. The official uses an instrument called a "go/no-go" gauge, in stock car language. The instrument has both a red and a green section on it. If the car height falls into the green section, the car is a legal height. If the car is measured in the red section, the height is too low and the car doesn't pass inspection.

Officials also open the hood of the car and check the engine and the other parts inside. Besides being inspected before the race, all competing cars can be inspected during or after the race as well.

Cars must pass a strict inspection before they can race.

*Opposite page: A pack of cars
battling for first place.*

-Race Day

On Sunday, the race teams arrive early and get all the equipment set up in the pits. Last minute repairs are made and all the parts of the car are checked and re-checked to make sure the car is ready to race. The car is then pushed out to the starting grid, the area on the track where the race will start. The order in which the cars line up was decided during qualifying, two days before. Marks on the starting grid show where the cars are to be placed. The pole sitter is placed in the front row in the inside lane. Usually the cars on the starting grid are covered with nylon covers to keep the interior cool.

A cart with a generator goes with every car. The generator provides power to preheat the oil and charge the battery. After the cars are on the starting grid, they will not be started until the race begins. The cars must stay in their places until the green flag waves and the start/finish line is crossed.

Opposite page: The start of the 1994 Winston Cup.

-Pit Stops

It is called a "pit stop" when the driver comes off the track during the race to have repairs made to the car. The driver goes down pit road to the spot where the pit crew is waiting. The pit crew must work together as a team to help get the driver back on the track as soon as possible. Every second a driver spends in the pits can cost the driver up to 17 car lengths on the track.

During a pit stop, tires are changed, fuel is added, the windshield is cleaned, and the driver is given a drink—all in less than 20 seconds! The fastest pits stops, for just a tire change, can take less than five seconds.

The pit crew practices pit stops many times before the actual race so that they can be as fast as possible. If one member of the team fails to do the job right, or bumps into another team member during a pit stop, it can cost the driver the race. It's a lot of pressure being on a pit crew. Pits stops can win or lose the race.

During a pit stop every second counts.

H C STORM SCHOOL

-Victory Lane

One of the ways race officials help make the race run smoothly is the use of different colored flags to direct the drivers on the race track. There are many flags used, each with a different meaning.

A green flag is used to signal the start of the race. When a driver sees the green flag waving, it means "GO." A yellow flag tells the drivers to be careful, stop passing, and that there might be a dangerous situation ahead. A red flag means the race is being stopped. Drivers are usually instructed to go into the pits or line up in a certain area when there is a red flag waving. A black flag pointed at a certain driver's car means the driver must go to the pits immediately. This flag means the car may not be safe to drive, or the driver is racing dangerously.

A white flag means that the leader of the race has started the last lap of the race. Only one lap to go! The flag most drivers want to see as they pass the start/finish line is the checkered flag. When the winning car crosses the finish line, this flag is waved and the crowd cheers!

When the winner and the second and third place finishers cross the finish line, the drivers are said to be in Victory Lane. The three drivers are presented with trophies and prize money. All the hours of preparation were well worth it. Now it's time to take the trophy, pack up the trailer, and head to the next race!

The first, second, and third place winners driving down victory lane.

–Glossary

Banked curve - Tracks which have very wide corners and are on a slope.

Body - Sheet metal panels of the car which fit over the chassis. The body is hand-crafted most of the time.

Chassis/roll cage - The frame of the car. The chassis is like a skeleton of the car.

Crew chief - The crew chief is in charge of organizing the pit crew, overseeing the preparation of the car, and working with the engine builder.

Daytona International Speedway - The most famous NASCAR track opened in 1959. The Daytona 500 races there. The track is 2-1/2 miles around.

Fuel cell - A large fuel tank used on stock cars.

Generator - The generator provides power to preheat the oil and charge the battery when the car is sitting on the starting grid before the race starts.

Inspection - All cars must pass requirements for the height, weight, and equipment used in and on the car. Cars are inspected before the race.

NASCAR - National Association for Stock Car Auto Racing, the rule-making organization for stock car racing.

Nomex - A fireproof material used for driving suits and other driver clothing.

Oval - A stock car track. Cars race around the track in one direction, counter-clockwise.

Pit crew - Members of the race team who help change tires and refuel during the race.

Pit stop - When the driver needs new tires or more fuel, the driver comes off the track during the race and makes a pit stop.

Pole sitter - The driver who had the fastest time during qualifying. This driver starts right in front at the race.

Qualifying - During qualifying, drivers compete for the fastest qualifying speed, which will determine their spot in the lineup of the race.

Quick-release - Equipment that is easy to remove. The steering wheel and driver's window net is quick-release.

Sponsors - Companies who help pay for the car.

Starting grid - The area on the track where the cars line up to begin the race.

Tire pressure - The amount of air that is put in the tire. In stock car racing, all four tires could have different amounts of air.

Victory Lane - Where the winner and the second and third place finishers go to when the race is over. This is where the trophies and prize money are awarded.

Winston Cup - The top NASCAR circuit, the 'major leagues' of stock car racing.

–Internet Sites

Formula 1 Links Heaven
http://ireland.iol.ie/~roym/
This site includes official sites, latest news, drivers, teams, computer games, circuits, mailing lists. This site has sound and video, very colorful and interactive.

Drag Racing on the net
http://www.lm.com/~hemi/
This is a cool and interactive sight with sound and fun photos.

Indyphoto.com
http://www.indyphoto.com/index.htm
This award winning site has excellent photographs of Indy Cars and it is updated on a regular basis.

MotorSports Image Online
http://www.msimage.com/index2.htm
This site gives you standings, results, schedules, teams, news, and a photo gallery.

Extreme Off-Road Racing
http://www.calpoly.edu/~jcallan/
This site has pre-runners, chat rooms, videos, racing pictures, wrecks, links, and much more extreme off-road racing stuff.

These sites are subject to change. Go to your favorite search engine and type in car racing for more sites.

Pass It On

Racing Enthusiasts: educate readers around the country by passing on information you've learned about car racing. Share your little-known facts and interesting stories. Tell others what your favorite kind of car is or who your favorite racer is. We want to hear from you!

To get posted on the ABDO & Daughters website E-mail us at "Sports@abdopub.com"

Visit the ABDO & Daughter website at www.abdopub.com

–Index